Weather Instruments

CONTENTS

Think About . . .

People in Science

Did You Know?

What Causes Earth's Weather?

Weather is what is happening in the air around Earth at a certain place and time. An ocean of air called the **atmosphere** surrounds Earth. The air layer closest to Earth is the **troposphere**. This is where most weather happens.

All weather can be traced to the effect of the sun's energy on the atmosphere. The sun is the main source of energy for Earth. Energy from the sun warms the land and water on Earth's surface. Then the surface warms the air above it.

The sun heats Earth unevenly. Cold **air masses** form over cold areas of Earth. Warm air masses form over warmer areas. Warm air is lighter than cold air, so warm air rises. Cold air moves in to take its place. This process keeps the air moving. It makes our weather change.

The atmosphere has layers. Some people call the troposphere the "weathersphere." This layer is where air masses mix and cause Earth's weather.

Weather has six main factors.

- air temperature
- air pressure
- wind
- clouds
- precipitation
- humidity

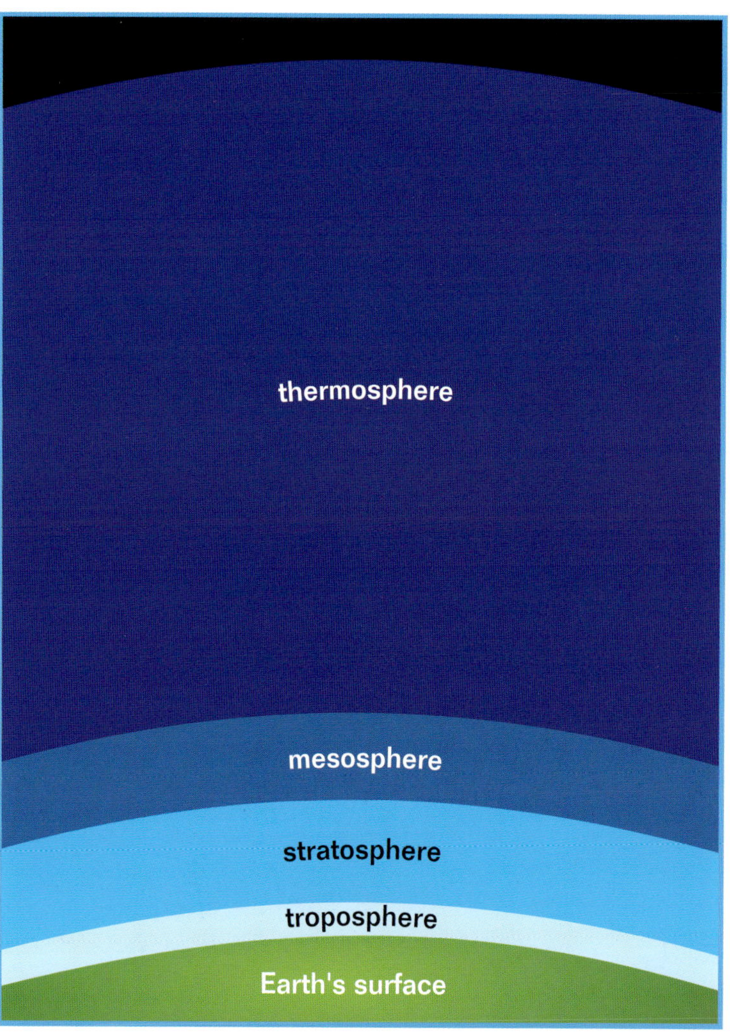

You can use your senses to observe some parts of the weather. You also can use special instruments.

How Do We Measure Air Temperature?

Suppose you're ready to leave for school. Do you need to wear a jacket? How will you decide? Knowing how warm or cold it is outside will help. That means you need to know the air **temperature** outdoors. Air temperature changes almost all the time. It is usually warmer during the day than it is at night.

A **thermometer** is an instrument that measures temperature. The numbers on a thermometer are the scale. The scale shows the temperature in degrees. Some thermometers use the **Fahrenheit** scale. Others show the **Celsius** scale. Many thermometers show both kinds of scales.

A thermometer in direct sunshine will not give a true reading. Sunlight hits the thermometer and heats it up. This makes the reading too high. Air temperature should be measured in the shade.

What is the reading on this dual-scale thermometer?

How Do We Measure Air Pressure?

The weight of the air around Earth presses down on Earth's surface. The pressing down of air is called **air pressure**. Air pressure lessens as you move higher up in the atmosphere. The higher you are, the less air is above you. Less air is pushing down on you, so the air pressure is lower.

Air temperature affects air pressure. As air warms up, its molecules move farther apart. The air becomes lighter and it rises. As warm air rises, it does not push down as hard on the Earth's surface. A low-pressure area forms.

When air cools, its molecules move closer together. It becomes heavier and sinks. Cold air pushes down on Earth's surface with more pressure than warm air. A high-pressure area forms where cool air sinks.

When the reading on a barometer changes, the weather usually changes too.

An instrument called a **barometer** measures air pressure. One kind of barometer contains a small box. Most of the air has been removed from the box. The weight of the outside air changes the shape of the box. Heavy air makes the box bend in. When the air pressure is lower, the box stretches out. Gears and levers send these changes to a pointer on a dial. The dial shows if the air pressure is high or low.

Air pressure at the top of a mountain is lower than it is at the base.

How Do We Measure Wind?

Think about blowing up a balloon. When you blow air into the balloon, you force air into it. The air inside the balloon now has high pressure. The air outside it has lower pressure. If you open the neck of the balloon, air rushes out. It moves from an area of high pressure to an area of low pressure.

A similar thing happens in the atmosphere. When warm air rises, cooler air moves in to take its place. Air moves from an area of high pressure to an area of low pressure. This moving air is **wind.**

An instrument called a **wind vane** shows what direction the wind is coming from. Letters on the wind vane show which way is north, south, east, and west. An arrow turns to point into the wind. If a wind vane's arrow is pointing north, that means wind is blowing from the north.

Wind vanes are often shaped like arrows or animals.

An **anemometer** measures wind speed. Wind pushes small cups and makes part of the anemometer spin. The faster the wind is blowing, the faster the cups spin. The anemometer counts how many turns the cups make in a certain time. The dial then shows the wind speed.

What Causes Clouds and Precipitation?

Water covers more than two-thirds of Earth's surface. This water is in rivers, lakes, and oceans. Heat energy from the sun warms up the water. It changes to a gas called **water vapor.** Water changing to a gas is called **evaporation.**

The water vapor rises into the atmosphere and cools. Then the water vapor changes back into tiny water drops. This change is called **condensation.** The tiny water drops form **clouds.** Sometimes clouds form very high in the air where it is even colder. These clouds can be made of tiny bits of ice.

Sometimes water drops or ice bits in clouds become too large and heavy to stay in the air. The water or ice falls back to Earth as rain or snow. Water or snow falling from clouds is called **precipitation.**

Some water from rain or melting snow seeps down into the ground. Some of it runs into rivers, lakes, and the oceans. Heat from the sun warms the water. Then the process starts again. This whole process is called the **water cycle.**

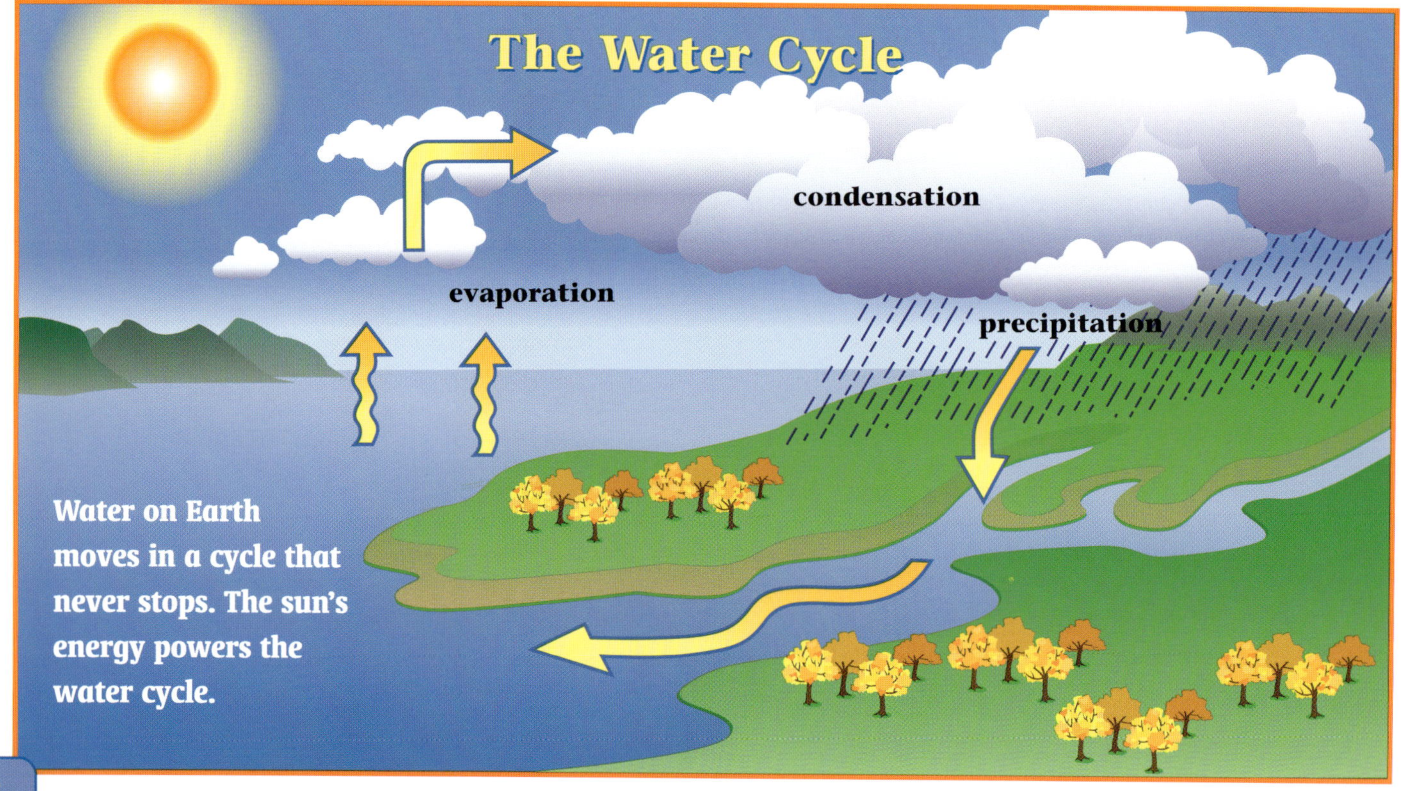

Water on Earth moves in a cycle that never stops. The sun's energy powers the water cycle.

In the desert, there is very little moisture in the air. The humidity is low.

On a wet-dry bulb hygrometer, the difference in the two temperatures tells the humidity.

How Do We Measure Humidity?

Air has different amounts of water vapor in it. Sometimes the air has only a little water vapor in it. The air feels dry. Other times air has a lot of water vapor in it. Then the air feels damp and sticky. Lots of water vapor rises from the ocean. That is why air near the coast may feel so humid.

The amount of water vapor in the air changes with the temperature. **Humidity** is a measure of how much water vapor is in the air.

A **hygrometer** is an instrument that measures humidity. One kind of hygrometer has two thermometers. The bottom of one is covered with wet cloth. Water evaporates from the cloth. It cools that thermometer. If the readings on the two thermometers are close, the air is humid. If the readings are far apart, the air is dry.

How Do We Measure Precipitation?

Rain, snow, sleet, and hail are all forms of precipitation. Rain falls when clouds form and large water drops become heavier and fall back down to Earth. Rain can be measured with a **rain gauge.** Ice crystals form in clouds that are very cold. If the air is below freezing all the way to the ground, it snows. You can measure snowfall with a ruler or meterstick.

Sometimes it's raining and a thick layer of cold air is close to the ground. Then raindrops can freeze into tiny pellets of ice, called sleet. If a thin layer of cold air is near the ground, the raindrops do not have time to freeze as they fall. The rain can freeze when it hits things at ground level. Freezing rain can break trees and power lines and make roads and sidewalks very slippery.

Most hail is smaller than a pea, but sometimes it can be as big as a softball.

A rain gauge collects rain. Markings on the side show how much rain has fallen.

Hail is made of balls of ice. It forms when rain freezes and is pushed higher in the air by strong winds in clouds. Each time a piece of hail is pushed up, another layer of ice is added. The hail keeps getting bigger and bigger. Finally, it gets too big for the wind to hold it in the air and the hail falls to the ground. Hail can damage cars, plants, and buildings.

Other Weather Instruments

If you watch the TV weather forecast, you may see a radar map that shows rain or snow. Radar is an instrument that sends signals into the air. These signals bounce off rain and snow. Radar tells us where rain or snow is falling and how it is moving. It helps us spot severe storms. It shows their direction and speed so we can prepare for bad weather.

Weather satellites in space take pictures of Earth's atmosphere and send them back to ground stations. The pictures show the parts of Earth that are covered by clouds. They also show how thick the clouds are. A series of pictures shows how the clouds are moving over time.

Satellite pictures of cloud cover let us track the movement of storms.

Scientists also use weather balloons to learn about weather high above Earth. Helium gas makes the balloons rise high into the air. Some balloons go higher than 25 kilometers (about 15 miles). They carry many instruments that gather weather data. The readings are sent back to Earth by radio.

Weather stations around the world launch weather balloons twice each day.

Scientists in the past experimented with many different temperature scales. Two main temperature scales are used today.

Gabriel Fahrenheit (1686–1736)

Gabriel Fahrenheit lived in The Netherlands most of his life. He is best known for the thermometers he invented. In 1724 he developed a new scale for measuring temperature. On this scale the freezing point of water is set at 32 degrees. The boiling point of water is 212 degrees. There are 180 degrees between these two points. The Fahrenheit scale is still used today in the United States.

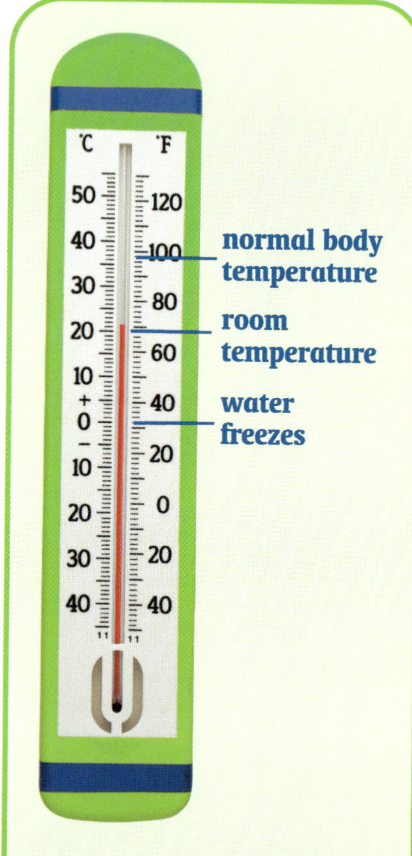

A hot day is 90° on the Fahrenheit scale. The same temperature is about 32° on the Celsius scale.

Anders Celsius (1701–1744)

Anders Celsius was a Swedish scientist who did experiments with temperature. In 1742 he developed a temperature scale. On his scale the freezing point of water is 0 degrees. The boiling point of water is 100 degrees. There are 100 degrees between these two points. Today the Celsius scale is used in most of the world and by scientists everywhere.

Sir Francis Beaufort (1774–1857)

Sir Francis Beaufort was an admiral in the British Navy. He studied the wind in the sails of his ship. In 1805 he came up with a wind scale. It showed how to tell wind speed by looking at ships' sails. Later the descriptions were changed so people on land could use the scale. What do you think the wind speed is today? Why?

Beaufort Scale

Force	Description	Effect	Wind Speed
0	calm	smoke rises	less than 1 mph
1	light air	smoke drifts	1–3 mph
2	light breeze	leaves rustle	4–7 mph
3	gentle breeze	leaves and twigs move	8–12 mph
4	moderate breeze	branches move; flags flap	13–18 mph
5	fresh breeze	small trees sway	19–24 mph
6	strong breeze	large branches move	25–31 mph
7	moderate gale	whole trees sway	32–38 mph
8	fresh gale	twigs break; walking is difficult	39–46 mph
9	strong gale	signs blow down; roofs are damaged	47–54 mph
10	whole gale	trees are uprooted	55–63 mph
11	storm	much general damage	64–73 mph
12	hurricane	buildings are destroyed	74 + mph

By studying the location of storms, meteorologists can help pilots fly around them.

Airport Meteorologists

Many of us want to know what the weather is like. But airplane pilots really *need* to know what the weather is like. Their planes fly in the air where our weather happens.

Many large airports have their own **meteorologists**. These scientists measure, record, and interpret weather data. They use many instruments to gather data over time. They study radar pictures and make **weather maps.** They study the warm and cold air masses. They look at the **fronts**—or lines between air masses. They look at how **cold fronts** and **warm fronts** are moving. They also look at where air masses are not moving, along **stationary fronts.**

If a big storm is coming, it might not be safe for planes to take off or land. Other airports might be closed because of storms.

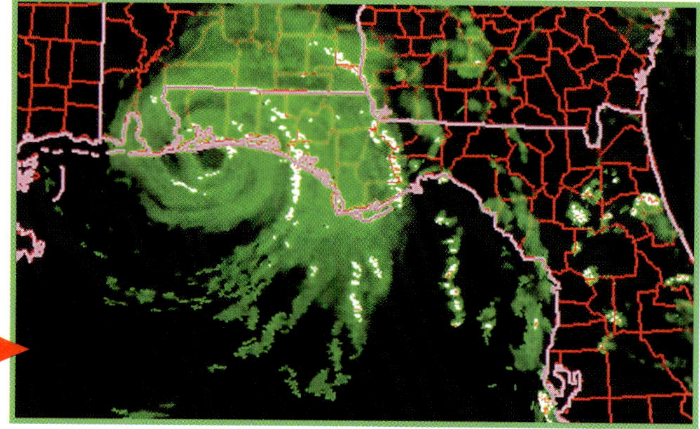
This radar picture shows a hurricane over the southeastern United States.

You can try to predict the weather yourself. Perhaps you have heard people say, "It looks like rain!" They probably are looking at the clouds in the sky. **Cirrus clouds** can mean cool, fair weather. But they might mean that precipitation or a storm is on the way. It depends on the direction of the wind. When **cumulus clouds** are small, they are called fair weather clouds. But if they are growing taller or darker, thunderstorms may be on the way. **Stratus clouds** often mean light rain.

Many clouds are variations of these three main types. Fog is a stratus-like cloud that forms at ground level. The tall, dark cumulus clouds that bring thunderstorms are called cumulonimbus clouds.

Cirrus clouds look feathery or wispy. They are the highest clouds. They are often made of ice crystals.

Cumulus clouds look heaped up and puffy.

Stratus clouds are layered, gray, and fairly close to the ground.

Did You Know?

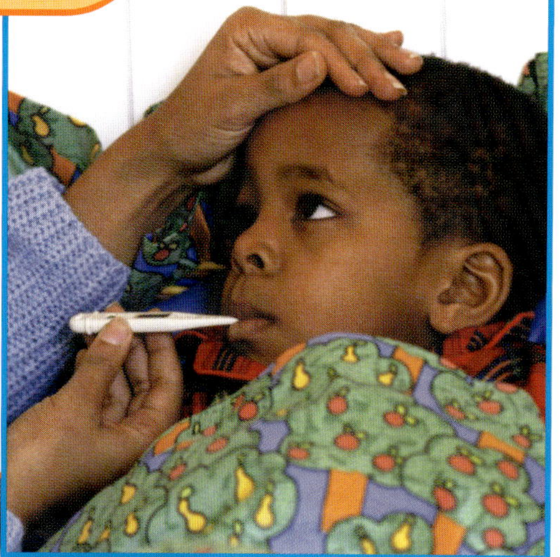

A digital thermometer tells if you are sick.

An outdoor dial thermometer shows the air temperature. Inside the thermometer is a special piece of metal. When the temperature goes up, the metal expands. It gets longer. When the temperature goes down, the metal contracts. It gets shorter. The changes in the metal move a pointer. It points to numbers on the dial.

A special kind of thermometer is used in making candy. It shows when the candy is ready for the next step.

How Thermometers Work

Have you seen a thermometer made of a glass tube with a colored liquid inside? The colored liquid is usually alcohol. When the temperature gets higher, the liquid expands. It takes up more space. It moves higher in the tube. When the temperature gets lower, the liquid contracts. It gets smaller. It drops lower in the tube.

The numbers and marks next to the glass tube show degrees. You look at the level of the liquid in the thermometer. Then you read the temperature.

About Wind Chill

Suppose the thermometer shows that it's 30°F outside. You know you should wear a warm jacket, a hat, and gloves. You put them on and go outside. Then you realize the wind is blowing really hard. It feels much, much colder than the reading on the thermometer. What you are feeling is the **wind chill**.

A nice breeze makes you feel cooler on a hot day. But when a strong wind blows and the temperature is cold, you really need to bundle up. Winter winds can be dangerous. They can make uncovered skin freeze.

At the South Pole the average temperature is –50°C (–58°F). The average wind speed is about 21 kilometers (about 13 miles) per hour. With the wind chill, it feels like –69°C (about –92°F).

temperature (°F)

wind speed (mph) / calm	30	25	20	15	10	5	0	-5	-10	-15	-20
5	25	19	13	7	1	-5	-11	-16	-22	-28	-34
10	21	15	9	3	-4	-10	-16	-22	-28	-35	-41
15	19	13	6	0	-7	-13	-19	-26	-32	-39	-45
20	17	11	4	-2	-9	-15	-22	-29	-35	-42	-48
25	16	9	3	-4	-11	-17	-24	-31	-37	-44	-51
30	15	8	1	-5	-12	-19	-26	-33	-39	-46	-53
35	14	7	0	-7	-14	-21	-27	-34	-41	-48	-55
40	13	6	-1	-8	-15	-22	-29	-36	-43	-50	-57
45	12	5	-2	-9	-16	-23	-30	-37	-44	-51	-58
50	12	4	-3	-10	-17	-24	-31	-38	-45	-52	-60

Wind Chill Chart

Find the temperature on the top and the wind speed on the left. Then find where the rows meet. This tells you how cold it feels because of the wind chill.

Glossary

air mass body of air that has about the same temperature and humidity throughout

air pressure force of the atmosphere pushing down on Earth

anemometer instrument used to measure the speed of the wind

atmosphere layer of air surrounding Earth

barometer instrument used to measure air pressure

Beaufort scale scale that relates wind speed to its effects on land and sea

Celsius type of temperature scale

cirrus cloud thin, feathery cloud made of ice crystals

cloud mass of tiny water droplets or ice particles in the air

cold front leading edge of a moving mass of cold air

condensation the process of a gas changing to a liquid

cumulus cloud puffy cloud

evaporation the process of a liquid changing to a gas

Fahrenheit type of temperature scale

front boundary between air masses with different temperatures

humidity the amount of water vapor in the air

hygrometer instrument used to measure humidity

meteorologist scientist who studies the weather

precipitation any form of water that falls from clouds to Earth

rain gauge instrument used to measure the amount of precipitation

stationary front place where a cold air mass and warm air mass meet, but neither moves

stratus cloud low, layered cloud

temperature measure of the amount of heat energy in a substance

thermometer instrument used to measure temperature

troposphere bottom layer of Earth's atmosphere where weather occurs

warm front the leading edge of a moving mass of warm air

water cycle constant movement of water from Earth to the atmosphere, and back to Earth

water vapor water in the form of a gas

weather what is happening in the atmosphere at a certain place and time

weather map map that shows weather conditions over a large area

wind moving air

wind chill how cold the air feels because of the wind

wind vane instrument used to tell the direction from which the wind is blowing